Chess Made Easy: New And Comprehensive Rules For Playing The Game Of Chess... - Primary Source Edition

Benjamin Franklin

CHESS MADE EASY.

NEW AND COMPREHENSIVE RULES

FOR PLAYING

The Game of Chess;

WITH EXAMPLES FROM

PHILIDOR, CUNNINGHAM,

&c. &c.

TO WHICH IS PREFIXED

A PLEASING ACCOUNT OF ITS ORIGIN;

SOME

INTERESTING ANECDOTES

OF SEVERAL

EXALTED PERSONAGES

WHO HAVE BEEN ADMIRERS OF IT;

AND THE

MORALS OF CHESS,

WRITTEN BY THE INGENIOUS AND LEARNED

DR. FRANKLIN.

A NEW EDITION, REVISED AND CORRECTED.

This Game an Indian Brahmin did invent,
The force of Eastern wisdom to express;
From thence the same to busy Europe sent;
The modern Lombards stil'd it pensive Chess.

DENHAM.

London:

PRINTED FOR J. HARRIS AND SON,

CORNER OF ST. PAUL'S CHURCH-YARD.

1820.

H. Bryer, Printer, Bridge-street,
Blackfriars, London.

ADVERTISEMENT.

IN this little Treatise, which the Editor offers with submission to the Public, he has endeavoured, and hopes with some degree of perspicuity, to point out the best method of attaining a knowledge of the agreeable and scientific *Game of Chess.*

Various have been the opinions of different writers, respecting its origin and antiquity; but none seem more clearly to prove it of Indian invention, than the Account prefixed, written by an ingenious Frenchman*. The Editor has also added a few anecdotes of some distinguished Personages, who were enthusiastic admirers of this amusement; together with the *Morals of Chess,* written by the late Dr. FRANKLIN, which he hopes will be deemed no improper appendages.

* M. FAVET.

~~~

The ANALYTICAL REVIEW of *August 1796*, speaks of this little Work in the following terms of approbation :—

" This small Volume appears very properly compiled to answer the purpose of an easy introduction to the knowledge of the Game of Chess. The introductory parts are curious, amusing, and instructive. The principles of the Game are concisely and clearly laid down, and five or six games are described with explanatory remarks; it will be an acceptable manual to those who are fond of this amusing exercise of the judgement."

~~~

ORIGIN

OF THE

GAME OF CHESS.

——————

IN the beginning of the fifth century of the christian era, there was in the Indies a very powerful prince, whose kingdom was situated towards where the Ganges discharges itself into the sea. He took to himself the proud title of king of the Indies; his father had forced a great number of sovereign princes to pay tribute to him, and submit themselves under his empire. The young monarch soon forgot, that kings ought to be the fathers of their people; that the subjects' love of their king is the only solid support of his throne; that his paternal care alone can truly attach the people to the prince who governs them, and that in them consists all his strength and power; that a king without subjects would only bear an empty title, and would have no real advantage above other men.

The Brahmins and Rajahs, *i. e.* the priests and nobility, represented all these things to the king of the Indies; but he, intoxicated with the idea of his grandeur, which he thought was not to be shaken, despised their wise remonstrances. Their complaints and representations continuing, he was offended, and to revenge his authority, which he thought despised by those who dared to disapprove his conduct, he caused them to be put to death in torments.

This example affrighted others. They were silent, and the prince, abandoned to himself, and what was more dangerous for him, and more terrible to his people, given up to the pernicious counsels of flatterers, was hurried on to the last excesses. The people were oppressed under a weight of insupportable tyranny; and the tributary princes, persuaded that the king of the Indies, in losing the love of his people, had lost the very essence of his power and strength, were preparing to throw off the yoke, and to carry the war into his estates. Then a Brahmin, or Indian philosopher, named Sissa, the son of Daher, touched with the misfortunes of his country, undertook to make the prince open his eyes upon the fatal effects which his conduct was likely to produce. But instructed by the example of those who had gone before him, he was sensible his lesson would not prove of any service, until the prince should make the application of it to himself, and not think that it was done by another. With this view, he invented the Game of Chess, where the king, although the most considerable of all the pieces, is both impotent to attack, as well as defend himself against his enemies, without the assistance of his subjects and soldiers.

The new game soon became famous; the king of the Indies heard of it, and would learn it. The Brahmin Sissa was pitched upon to teach it him; and under the pretext of explaining the rules of the game, and shewing him the skill required to make use of the other pieces, for the king's defence, he made him perceive and relish important truths, which he had hitherto refused to hear. The king, endued naturally with understanding and virtuous sentiments, which the pernicious maxims of his flatterers and courtiers could not wholly extinguish, made an application himself of the Brahmin's lessons; and now convinced that in the people's love of their king consisted all his strength, he altered his conduct, and prevented the misfortunes that threatened him.

The prince was sensibly touched, and gratefully left to the Brahmin the choice of his reward. He desired that the number of grains of corn, which the number of the squares of the chess-board should produce, might be given him,—one for the first, two for the second, four for the third, and so on, doubling always to the sixty-fourth.

The king astonished at the seeming modesty and reasonableness of the demand, granted it immediately, and without examination ; but when his treasurers had made the calculation, they found that the king had engaged himself in a grant, for the performance whereof neither all his treasures, nor his vast dominions were sufficient. Then the Brahmin laid hold of this opportunity, to give him to understand, of what importance it was to kings to be upon their guard against those who are always about them, and how much they ought to be afraid of their ministers abusing their best intentions.

The game of chess was not long confined to India, it passed into Persia, during the reign of Cosores. The Persians looked upon it as a game to be made use of in all countries, to instruct kings, at the same time that it amused them, as the name which they gave it signifies, schertrengi, or schatrak. The game of schah, or king.

The names of many of the pieces of this game, which have no reasonable signification, but in the Eastern languages, confirm the opinion we propose, of its Eastern original. The second piece of chess, after the king, is now called the queen. The old French authors call it fierce, fierche, and fierge, or fiercir. Corruptions of the Latin fiercia, derived from the Persian ferz or firzin, the name of that piece in Persic; and signifies a minister or vizir. Of the word fierge, they have made vierge, virgo, and afterwards lady, or queen. The resemblance of the words made this change very easy; and it seemed so much the more reasonable, because that piece is placed next to the king, and at its first moves, like the pawns, could only move two steps, which made it one of the least considerable of the board, as the authors of two ancient treatises of the game of chess acknowledge.

The constraint upon the lady of chess was displeasing to our forefathers. They looked upon it as a sort of slavery, more suitable to the jealousy of the Eastern people, than to the liberty which ladies have always enjoyed amongst us. They extended, therefore, the steps and prerogatives of that piece, and in consequence of the gallantry so natural to the Western people, the lady became the most considerable piece of all the game.

There was still an absurdity in this metamorphosis of the firzim or vizir into queen, and this incongruity remains to the present day, without our taking notice of it.

When a pawn, or a simple soldier, has traversed through the enemy's battalions, and penetrated so far as the last line of the board, he is not allowed to return back, but is honoured with the step and prerogatives of the queen.

If the firzim or fierge be a vizir, a first minister, or a general of an army, we can easily comprehend how a pawn or a simple soldier may be elevated to their rank, in recompence of the valour with which he has pierced through the enemy's battalions. But if the fierge be a lady, a queen, or the king's wife, by what odd metamorphosis does the pawn change his sex and become a woman, that was a soldier before? And how do they make him marry the king, in recompence of that valour of which he has given such proofs. This absurdity proves, that the second piece of chess has been *mal à propos* called lady or queen; for what king ever became so enamoured of his first minister as to marry him, and take him for better for worse, until death do them part.

The third piece of chess, which we call the bishop; the French, fool; the Spaniards alferez; and the Italians, alfiere: serjeant, in the East; was in the figure of an elephant, and whose name it bore. The knight, which is the fourth piece, has the same name and figure every where. The fifth piece, which we call the rook, and the French, tour, is called by the Eastern people, the rohk; and the Indians make it of the figure of a camel, mounted by an horseman, with a bow and arrow in his hand.

The name of rohk, which is common both to the Persians and Indians, signifies, in the language of the East, a sort of camel used in war, and placed upon the wings of their armies, by way of light horse. The rapid motion of the piece, which jumps from one end of the board to the other, agrees so much the better with this idea of it, as at first it was the only piece who had that motion.

The king, queen, and pawn made but one step; the bishop but two, as well as the knight, neither of them going farther than the third square, including that which they quitted. The rook alone was unbounded in his course, which may agree to the lightness of the dromedary, but in no ways to the immobility of towers or fortresses, the figures of which we generally give to those pieces. The sixth, and last piece, is the pawn, or common-soldier, which has been suffered to change.

The Chinese have made some alterations in this game; they have introduced new pieces, under the name of cannons or mortars, the use of artillery and powder having been long known to them, before it was discovered by the Europeans. Tamerlane made yet greater changes in this game; and by the new pieces which he invented, and the motion he gave them, he increased the difficulty of a game already too complicated to be looked upon as an amusement; but these additions have not been approved of; and the ancient manner of playing, each with sixteen pieces only, and upon a board of sixty-four squares, has taken place again.

ANECDOTES

OF THE

GAME OF CHESS.

In the second volume, octavo, of the Modern Universal History, I find, " Al Amin, Khalif of Bagdad, and his freedman Kuthar, were playing at chess without the least apprehension of impending danger, when Al Mamun's forces pushed the siege of Bagdad with so much vigour, that the city was upon the point of being carried by assault." Dr. Hyde quotes an Arabic History of the Saracens, which says, that on this occasion he cried out, when he was warned of his danger, " Let me alone! for I seek Checkmate against Kuthar." It is farther recounted of him that " he commanded the different provinces of the empire, to send to his court all such persons as were most expert at chess, to whom he allowed pensions, and passed the most considerable part of his time among them." This was about the year 808.

In a battle between the French and English, in the year 1117, an English knight seizing the bridle of Louis le Gros, and crying to his comrades, *the king is taken;* the prince struck him to the ground with his sword, saying, "*Ne sçais tu pas qu' aux echecs on ne prend pas le roi?*"—"Dost thou not know that at chess the kings are never taken?" The meaning of which is this: At the game of chess, when the king is reduced to that pass, that there is no way for him to escape, the game ends, because the royal piece is not to be exposed even to an imaginary affront.

Ben-Ziad, caliph of Mecca, was very fond of chess. "Is it not extraordinary," said he to the favourite he was playing with, "that sixteen pieces, placed on so small a plane as this chess-board, should give me more trouble to manage, than so many millions of men, that cover the immense surface of my empire?"

The following remarkable anecdote we have from Dr. Robertson, in his history of Charles the Fifth: John Frederick, Elector of Saxony, having been taken prisoner by Charles, was condemned to death; the decree was intimated to him while at chess with Ernest of Brunswick, his fellow-prisoner. After a short pause, and making some reflections on the irregularity of the emperor's proceedings, he turned

to his antagonist, whom he challenged to finish
the game. He played with his usual ingenuity
and attention, and having beat Ernest, ex-
pressed all the satisfaction that is commonly
felt on gaining such victories. He was not,
however, put to death, but set at liberty after
five years confinement.

~~~

In the chronicle of the Moorish kings of
Grenada, we find it related, that in 1396, Mehmed Balba seized upon the crown in prejudice
of his elder brother, and passed his life in one
continued round of disasters. His wars with
Castile were invariably unsuccessful; and his
death was occasioned by a poisoned vest.
Finding his case desperate, he dispatched an
officer to the port of Solobrena, to put his brother Jusaf to death, lest that prince's adherents
should form any obstacle to his son's succes-
sion. The alcade found the prince playing at
chess with an *alfayue* or priest. Jusaf begged
hard for two hours' respite, which was denied
him. At last, with great reluctance, the officer
permitted him to finish his game, but before it
was finished, a messenger arrived with the
news of the death of Mehmed, and the unani-
mous election of Jusaf to the crown.

Charles the First was at chess, when news was brought of the final intention of the Scots to sell him to the English; but so little was he discomposed by this alarming intelligence, that he continued his game with the utmost composure, so that no person could have known that the letter he had received had given him information of any thing remarkable.

~~~

King John was playing at chess when the deputies came to acquaint him, that their city was besieged by Philip Augustus, but he would not hear them until he had finished his game.

~~~

When Charles the Twelfth was at Bender, Voltaire says, " for his only amusement, he played sometimes at chess. If little things paint men, I may be allowed to mention, that he always made the king march at that game; he made use of it more than of any of the other pieces, and by that means he lost every game." And again, when he was besieged by the Turks, in the house in which he had shut himself up, near Bender, after he had well barricaded his house, he sat down coolly to play at chess with his favourite *Grothusen*, as if every thing had been in profound security.

Mr. Philidor saw, in 1747, at Rotterdam, in the possession of a coffee house keeper, a set of chess-men which were made for Prince Eugene. They were three inches in height, of solid silver, chased, not different in colour, but sufficiently distinguished, by one side representing an European, and the other an Asiatic army. Mr. Twiss says, the most valuable chess-men he had seen are at Rotterdam. They were made by Vander Werf, (the celebreted painter) who employed the leisure hours of eighteen years in carving them. The pieces are three inches high, and the pawns two. Half the number are of box, and the other half ebony. They are all, except the castles, busts on pedestals : the kings are decorated with a lion's skin. The bishops have fools-caps with bells ; the knight's are horse's heads ; the pawns as well as the pieces are all different, being eight negroes, and eight whites of various ages.

~~~

Mr. Cox, who was in Russia, in 1772, says, " Chess is so common in Russia, that during our continuance at Moscow, I scarcely entered into any company where parties were not engaged in that diversion ; and I very frequently observed in my passage through the streets, the tradesmen and common people playing it before the doors of their shops or houses. The Russians are esteemed great proficients in chess: with them the queen has, in addition to the other moves, that of the knight, which according to Philidor, spoils the game; but which certainly renders it more complicated and difficult, and of course more interesting. The Russians have also another method of playing the game of chess, namely, with four persons at the same time, two against two: and for this purpose, the board is larger than usual, contains more men, and is provided with a greater number of squares. I was informed that this method was more difficult, but far more agreeable than the common game.

~~~

The Editor could have added many others of a similar nature, but they would have increased the size of the book beyond what he intended, he therefore concludes what may be deemed the introductory part of it, with

THE

MORALS OF CHESS.

BY DR. FRANKLIN.

THE game of chess is not merely an idle amusement. Several very valuable qualities of the mind, useful in the course of human life, are to be acquired or strengthened by it, so as to become habits, ready on all occasions. For life is a kind of chess, in which we have often points to gain, and competitors or adversaries to contend with, and in which there is a vast variety of good and ill events, that are, in some degree, the effects of prudence or the want of it. By playing at chess, then, we may learn,

I. *Foresight*, which looks a little into futurity, and considers the consequences that may attend an action : for it is continually occurring to the player, " If I move this piece, what will be the advantage of my new situation ? What use can my adversary make of it to annoy me ? What other moves can I make to support it, and to defend myself from his attacks ?"

II. *Circumspection,* which surveys the whole chess-board, or scene of action, the relations of the several pieces, and situations, the dangers they are respectively exposed to, the several possibilities of their aiding each other, the probabilities that the adversary may take this or that move, and attack this or the other piece, and what different means can be used to avoid his stroke, to turn its consequences against him.

III. *Caution,* not to make our moves too hastily. This habit is best acquired by observing strictly the laws of the game, such as, "If you touch a piece, you must move it somewhere; if you set it down, you must let it stand:" and it is therefore best that these rules should be observed, as the game thereby becomes more the image of human life, and particularly of war; in which, if you have incautiously put yourself into a bad and dangerous position, you cannot obtain your enemy's leave to withdraw your troops, and place them more securely, but you must abide all the consequences of your rashness.

And lastly, we learn by chess the habit of *not being discouraged by present bad appearance in the state of our affairs,* the habit of *hoping for a favourable change,* and that of *persevering in the search of resources.* The game is so full of events, there is such a variety of turns in it, the fortune of it is so subject to sudden vicissitudes, and one so frequently, after long contemplation, discovers the means of extricating oneself from a supposed insurmountable difficulty, that one is encouraged to continue the contest to the last, in hopes of victory by our own skill, or at least of giving a stale mate, by the negligence of our adversary. And whoever considers, what in chess he often sees instances of, that particular pieces of success are apt to produce presumption, and its consequent inattention, by which the loss may be recovered, will learn not to be too much discouraged by the present success of his adversary, nor to despair of final good fortune, upon every little check he receives in the pursuit of it.

That we may, therefore, be induced more frequently to choose this beneficial amusement, in preference to others, which are not attended with the same advantages, every circumstance which may increase the pleasures of it should be regarded; and every action or word that is unfair, disrespectful, or that in any way may give uneasiness, should be avoided, as contrary to the immediate intention of both the players, which is, to pass the time agreeably.

Therefore, first, If it is agreed to play according to the strict rules; then those rules are to be exactly observed by both parties, and should not be insisted on for one side, while deviated from by the other—for this is not equitable.

Secondly, If it is agreed not to observe the rules exactly, but one party demands indulgences, he should then be as willing to allow them to the other.

Thirdly, No false move should ever be made to extricate yourself out of a difficulty, or to gain an advantage. There can be no pleasure in playing with a person once detected in such unfair practices.

Fourthly, If your adversary is long in playing, you ought not to hurry him, or express any uneasiness at his delay. You should not sing, nor whistle, nor look at your watch, nor take up a book to read, nor make a tapping with your feet on the floor, or with your fingers upon the table, nor do any thing that may disturb his attention. For all these things displease ; and they do not shew your skill in playing, but your craftiness or your rudeness.

Fifthly, You ought not to endeavour to amuse and deceive your adversary, by pretending to have made bad moves, and saying that you have now lost the game, in order to make him secure and careless, and inattentive to your schemes : for this is fraud and deceit, not skill in the game.

Sixthly, You must not, when you have gained a victory, use any triumphing or insulting expression, nor show too much pleasure ; but endeavour to console your adversary, and make him less dissatisfied with himself, by every kind of civil expression that may be used with truth, such as, " You understand the game better than I, but you are a little inattentive ;" or, " You had the best of the game, but something happened to divert your thoughts, and that turned it in my favour."

Seventhly, If you are a spectator while others play, observe the most perfect silence, for if you give advice you offend both parties ; him against whom you give it, because it may cause the loss of his game; him in whose favour you give it; because, though it be good, and he follows it, he loses the pleasure he might have had, if you had permitted him to think until it had occurred to himself. Even after a move or moves, you must not, by replacing the pieces, shew how it might have been placed better; for that displeases, and may occasion disputes and doubts about their true situation. All talking to the players lessens or diverts their attention, and is therefore unpleasing. Nor should you give the least hint to either party, by any kind of noise or motion. If you do, you are unworthy to be a spectator. If you have a mind to exercise or shew your judgment, do it in playing your own game, when you have an opportunity, not in criticising, or meddling with, or counselling the play of others.

Lastly, if the game is not to be played rigorously, according to the rules above mentioned, then moderate your desire of victory over your adversary, and be pleased with one over yourself. Snatch not eagerly at every advantage offered by his unskilfulness or inattention; but point out to him kindly, that by such a move he places or leaves a piece in danger and unsupported; that by another he will put his king in a perilous situation, &c. By this generous civility (so opposite to the unfairness above forbidden) you may, indeed, happen to lose the game to your opponent, but you will win what is better, his esteem, his respect, and his affection; together with the silent approbation and good will of impartial spectators.

A NEW AND COMPREHENSIVE TREATISE

ON THE

GAME OF CHESS.

THIS ingenious game is performed with different pieces of wood, on a board divided into sixty-four squares or houses; in which chance has so small a share, that it may be doubted whether a person ever lost a game, but by his own fault.

Each gamester has eight dignified pieces, viz. a king, a queen, two bishops, two knights, and two rooks; also eight pawns; all of which, for distinction sake, are painted of two different colours, as white and black.

As to the disposition on the board: the white king is to be placed on the fourth black house from the corner of the board, in the first and lower rank; and the black king is to be placed on the fourth white house, on the opposite, or adversary's end of the board; the queens are to be placed next to the kings, on houses of their own colour. Next to the king and queen on each hand, place the two bishops; next to them the two knights; and last of all, on the corners of the board, the two rooks. As to the pawns, they are placed without distinction, on the second rank of the house, one before each of the dignified pieces.

Having thus disposed of the men, the on-set is commonly begun by the pawns, which march straight forward in their own file, one house at a time, except the first moves, when it can advance two houses, but never moves backwards. The manner of their taking the adversary's men is sideways, in the next house forwards, where having made captures of the enemy, they move forward as before. The rook goes forward, or crossways, through the whole file and back again: the knight skips backward and forward, to the next house, save one of a different colour, with a sidling march or slope; and thus kills his enemies that fall in his way, or guard his friends that may be exposed on that side: the bishop walks always in the same colour of the field that he is placed in at first, forward and back-ward, aslope or diagonally, as far as he lists: the queen's walk is more universal, as she takes all the steps of the before-mentioned pieces, excepting that of the knight; and as to the king's motion, it is one house at a time, and that either forward, backward, sloping or sideways.

As to the value of the different pieces; next to the king is the queen; after her the rooks; then the bishops; and last of the dignified pieces comes the knight. The difference of the worth of pawns is not so great as that of noblemen; only it must be observed, that the king's bishop's pawn is the best in the field; and therefore the skilful gamester, will be careful of him. It ought also to be observed, that, whereas any man may be taken when he falls within the reach of any of the adversary's pieces; it is otherwise with the king, who in such a case is only to be saluted with the word *check*, warning him of his danger, out of which it is absolutely necessary that he move; and if it so happens that he cannot move without exposing himself to the like inconveniency, it is check-mate, and the game is lost; the rules of the game are as follow.

I. In order to begin the game, the pawns must be moved before the pieces, and afterwards the pieces must be brought out to support them. The king's, queen's, and bishop's pawns should be moved first, that the game may be well opened. The pieces must not be played out early in the game, because the player may thereby lose his move; but above all, the game should be well arranged before the queen is played out. Useless checks should also be avoided, unless some advantage is to be gained by them, because the move may be lost, if the adversary can either take or drive the piece away.

II. If the game is crowded, the player will meet with obstructions in moving his pieces; for which reason he should exchange pieces or pawns, and castle* his king as soon as it is convenient, endeavouring at the same time to crowd the adversary's game, which may be done by attacking his pieces with the pawns, if the adversary should move his pieces out too soon.

III. The men should be so guarded by one another, that if a man should be lost, the player may have it in his power to take one

---

* *Castle his king*, is to cover his king with a castle; this is done by a certain move which each player has a right to, whenever he thinks proper.

of the adversary's in return : and if he can take a superior piece, in lieu of that which he has lost, it would be an advantage, and distress the adversary.

IV. The adversary's king should never be attacked without a force sufficient ; and if the player's king should be attacked without having it in his power to attack the adversary's, he should offer to make an exchange of pieces, which may cause the adversary to lose a move.

V. The board should be looked over with attention, and the men reconnoitred, so as to beware of any stroke that the adversary might attempt in consequence of his last move. If by counting as many moves forward as possible, the player has a prospect of success, he should not fail doing it, and even sacrifice a piece or two to accomplish his end.

VI. No man should be played till the board is thoroughly examined, that the player may defend himself against any move the adversary may have in view ; neither should the attack be made till the consequences of the adversary's next move are considered ; and when an attack may with safety be made, it should be pursued, without catching at any bait that might be thrown out, in order for the adversary to gain a move, and thereby cause the design to miscarry.

VII. The queen should never stand in such a manner before the king, that the adversary, by bringing a rook, or a bishop, could check the king if she were not there; as it might be the loss of the queen.

VIII. The adversary's knight should never be suffered to check the king and queen, or king and rook, or queen and rook, or the two rooks at the same time; especially if the knight is properly guarded; because in the two first cases, the king being forced to go out of check, the queen, or the rook must be lost; and in the two last cases a rook must be lost, at least, for a worse piece.

IX. The player should take care, that no guarded pawn of the adversary's fork two of his pieces.

X. As soon as the kings have castled on different sides of the board, the pawns on that side of the board should be advanced upon the adversary's king, and the pieces, especially the queen and rook, should be brought to support them; and the three pawns belonging to the king that is castled, must not be moved.

XI. The more moves a player can have, as it were in ambuscade, the better; that is to say, the queen, bishop, or rook, is to be placed behind a pawn, or piece, in such a position, as that upon playing that pawn or piece, a check is discovered upon the adversary's king, by which means a piece of some advantage is often gained.

XII. An inferior piece should never be guarded with a superior, when a pawn would answer the same purpose; for this reason, the superior piece may remain out at play, neither should a pawn be guarded with a piece, when a pawn would do as well.

XIII. A well supported pawn, that is passed, often costs the adversary a piece; and when a pawn or any other advantage, is gained without endangering the loss of the move, the player should make as frequent exchanges of pieces as he can. The advantage of a passed pawn is this, for example: if the player and his adversary have each three pawns upon the board, and no piece, and the player has one of his pawns on one side of the board, and the other two on the other side, and the adversary's three pawns are opposite to the players two pawns, he should march with his king as soon as he can, and take the adversary's pawns: if the adversary goes with his king to support them, the player should go to the queen with his single pawns; and then if the adversary goes to hinder him, he should take the adversary's pawns, and move the others to queen.*

XIV. When the game is near finished, each party having only three or four pawns on each side of the board, the king must endeavour to gain the move in order to win the game. For instance, when the player brings his king opposite to the adversary's, with only one square between, he will gain the move.

XV. If the adversary has his king, and one pawn on the board, and the player has only his king, he cannot lose the game, provided he brings his king opposite to the adversary's when the adversary is directly before, or on

---

* *To queen,* is to make a queen; that is to move a pawn into the adversary's back-row, which is the rule at this game, when the original one is lost.

one side of his pawn, and there is only one square between the kings.

XVI. If the adversary has a bishop, and one pawn on the rook's line, and this bishop is not of the colour that commands the corner square the pawn is going to, and the player has only his king, if he can get into that corner, he cannot lose; but on the contrary may win by a *stale.*＊

XVII. If the player has greatly the disadvantage of the game, having only his queen left in play, and his king happens to be in a position to win, as above mentioned, he should keep giving check to the adversary's king, always taking care not to check him, where he can interpose any of his pieces that make the stale; by so doing he will at last force the adversary to take his queen, and then he will win the game by being in a stale mate.

XVIII. The player should never cover a check with a piece that a pawn pushed upon it may take, for fear of getting only the pawn in exchange for the piece.

＊ When the king is blocked up so as to have no move at all.

XIX. A player should never crowd his adversary up with pieces, for fear of giving a stale mate inadvertently; but always should leave room for his king to move.

By way of corroborating what has been already said with respect to this game, it is necessary to warn a player against playing a timid game. He should never be too much afraid of losing a rook for an inferior piece; because although a rook is a better piece than any other, except the queen, it seldom comes into play to be of any great use till the end of the game; for which reason it is often better to have an inferior piece in play, than a superior one to stand still, or moving to no great purpose. If a piece is moved, and is immediately drove away by a pawn, it may be reckoned a bad move, because the adversary gains a double advantage over the player, in advancing at the same time the other is made to retire, although the first move may not seem of consequence between equal players, yet a move or two more lost after the first makes the game scarcely recoverable.

There never wants variety in this game, provided the pieces have been brought out regular; but if otherwise, it often happens that a player has scarcely any thing to play.

Many indifferent players think nothing of the pawns, whereas three pawns together are strong, but four, which constitute a square, with the assistance of other pieces well managed, make an invincible strength, and in all probability may produce a queen when very much wanted. It is true, that two pawns with a space between are no better than one; and if there should be three over each other in a line, the game cannot be in a worse way. This shews the pawns are of great consequence, provided they are kept close together.

Some middling players are very apt to risque losing the game, in order to recover a piece: This is a mistake; for it is much better to give up a piece, and attack the enemy in another quarter; by so doing, the player has a chance of snatching a pawn or two from, or gaining some advantage over the adversary, whilst his attention is taken up in pursuing this piece.

If the queen and another piece are attacked at the same time, and that by removing the queen, the piece must be lost; provided two pieces can be gained in exchange for the queen, the queen should be given up, it being the difference of three pieces, and consequently more than the value of the queen. By losing the queen the game is not thrown into that disorder which it would otherwise have been; in this case it would be judicious to give the queen for even a piece, or a pawn or two; it being well known among good players, that he who begins the attack, and cannot maintain it, being obliged to retire, generally loses the game.

A player should never be fond of changing without reason; because the adversary, if he is a good player, will ruin his situation, and gain a considerable advantage over him; but rather than lose a move, when a player is stronger than his adversary, it is good play to change, for he thereby increases his strength.

When the game is almost drawn to a conclusion, the player should recollect, that his king is a capital piece, and consequently should keep him in motion; by so doing he generally gets the move, and often the game.

As the queen, rook, and bishop, operate at a distance, it is not always necessary in

D

the attack to have them near the adversary's king.

If a man can be taken with different pieces, the player should take his time, and consider which of those pieces is the best to take it with.

If a piece can be taken almost at any time, the player should not be in a hurry about it, but try to make a good move elsewhere, before he takes it.

A player should be cautious how he takes his adversary's pawn with his king, as it often happens to be a safeguard to it.

After all that has been said, it is still necessary to advise those who would play well at this game, to be very cool and attentive to the matter in question ; for it is impossible that any person in the universe can be capable of playing at chess, if their thoughts are employed elsewhere.

The laws of the game are

I. If a player touches a man, he must play it ; and if he quits it he cannot recal it.

II. If by mistake, or otherwise, a false move is played, and the adversary takes no notice of it till he has played his next move, it cannot be recalled by either of the parties.

III. If a player misplaces the men, and he plays two moves, it is at the option of the adversary to permit him to begin the game or not.

IV. If the adversary plays, or discovers a check to a player's king, and gives no notice of it, the player may let him stand still till he does.

V. After the king is moved, a player cannot castle.

Several inventions, similar to this game, are mentioned by Mr. Twiss, and others, but all allow them to be of so complicated a nature, as to make them unworthy the attention of its admirers in this country; the Editor, therefore, concludes his little Treatise with a few examples from Mr. PHILIDOR, of whose celebrity as a chess player in this, and other countries, it is not necessary for him to speak.

Mr. PHILIDOR's METHOD

OF

PLAYING.

~~~

GAME THE FIRST.

WITH

Reflections on the most material Moves; and two Back Games; one beginning from the 12th, and the second from the 37th Move of this Game.

~~~~

1.

White. The king's pawn two steps.

Black. The same.

2.

W. The king's bishop at his queen's bishop's fourth square.

B. The same.

3.

W. The queen's bishop's pawn one move.

B. The king's knight at his bishop's third square.

4.

W. The queen's pawn two moves *(a)*.

B. The pawn takes it.

5.

W. The pawn retakes the pawn *(b)*.

B. The king's bishop at his queen's knight's third square *(c)*.

6.

W. The queen's knight at his bishop's third square.

B. The king castles.

7.

W. The king's knight at his king's second square *(d)*.

B. The queen's bishop's pawn one move.

8.

W. The king's bishop at his queen's third square *(e)*.

B. The queen's pawn two moves.

9.

W. The king's pawn one move.

B. The king's knight at his king's square.

10.

W. The queen's bishop at his king's third square.

B. The king's bishop's pawn one move *(f)*.

11.

W. The queen at her second square *(g)*.

B. The king's bishop's pawn takes the pawn *(h)*.

12.

W. The queen's pawn retakes it.

B. The queen's bishop at his king's third square (i).

13.

W. The king's knight at his king's bishop's fourth square (k).

B. The queen at her king's second square.

14.

W. The queen's bishop takes the black bishop (l).

B. The pawn takes the bishop.

15.

W. The king castles with his rook (m).

B. The queen's knight at his queen's second square.

16.

W. The knight takes the black bishop.

B. The queen takes the knight.

17.

W. The king's bishop's pawn two steps.

B. The king's knight at his queen's bishop's second square.

18.

W. The queen rook at its king's place.

B. The king's knight's pawn one move (n).

19.

W. The king's rook's pawn one move (o).

B. The queen's pawn one move.

20.

W. The knight at his king's fourth square.

B. The king's rook's pawn one move *(p)*.

21.

W. The queen's knight's pawn one move.

B. The queen's rook's pawn one move.

22.

W. The king's knight's pawn two steps.

B. The king's knight at his queen's fourth square.

23.

W. The knight at his king's knight's third square *(q)*.

B. The king's knight at the white king's third square *(r)*.

24.

W. The queen's rook takes the knight.

B. The pawn takes the rook.

25.

W. The queen takes the pawn.

B. The queen's rook takes the pawn of the opposite rook.

26.

W. The rook at his king's place *(s)*.

B. The queen takes the white queen's knight's pawn.

27.

W. The queen at her king's fourth square.

B. The queen at her king's third square *(t)*.

28.

W. The king's bishop's pawn one move.

B. The pawn takes it.

29.

W. The pawn takes again *(u)*.

B. The queen at the fourth square *(w)*.

30.

W. The queen takes the queen.

B. The pawn takes the queen.

31.

W. The bishop takes the pawn in his way.

B. The knight at his third square.

32.

W. The king's bishop's pawn one move *(x)*.

B. The queen's rook at the white queen's knight's second square.

33.

W. The bishop at his queen's third square.

B. The king at his bishop's second square.

34.

W. The bishop at the black king's bishop's fourth square.

B. The knight at the white queen's bishop's fourth square.

35.

W. The knight at the black king's rook's fourth square.

B. The king's rook gives check.

36.

W. The bishop covers the check.

B. The knight at the white queen's second square.

37.

W. The king's pawn gives check.

B. The king at his knight's third square *(y)*.

38.

W. The king's bishop's pawn one move.

B. The rook at its king's bishop's square.

39.

W. The knight gives check at the fourth square of his king's bishop.

B. The king at his knight's second square.

40.

W. The bishop at the black king's rook's fourth square.

B. Plays any where, the white pushes to queen.

FIRST BACK GAME;

OR,

Continuation of the preceding Game from the 12th Move.

~~~~~~~~

12.

W. The king's pawn retakes it.

B. The king's bishop takes the white queen's bishop.

13.

W. The queen takes the bishop.

B. The queen's bishop at his king's third square.

14.

W. The king's knight at his king's bishop's fourth square.

B. The queen at her king's second square.

15.

W. The knight takes the bishop.

B. The queen takes the knight.

16.

W. The king castles his rook.

B. The queen's knight at his queen's second square.

17.

W. The king's bishop's pawn two moves.

B. The king's knight's pawn one move.

18.

W. The king's rook's pawn one move.

B. The king's knight at his second square.

19.

W. The king's knight's pawn two steps.

B. The queen's bishop's pawn one move.

20.

W. The knight at his king's second square.

B. The queen's pawn one move.

21.

W. The queen at her second square.

B. The queen's knight at his third square.

22.

W. The knight at his king's knight's third square.

B. The queen's knight at his queen's fourth square.

23.

W. The queen's rook at its king's square.

B. The queen's knight at the white king's third square.

24.

W. The rook takes the knight.

B. The pawn takes the rook.

25.

W. The queen takes the pawn.

B. The queen takes the white queen's rook's pawn.

26.

W. The king's bishop's pawn one move.

B. The queen takes the pawn.

27.

W. The king's bishop's pawn one move.

B. The knight at his king's square.

28.

W. The king's knight's pawn one move.

B. The queen at the white queen's fourth square.

29.

W. The queen takes the queen.

B. The pawn takes the queen.

30.

W. The king's pawn one move.

B. The knight at his queen's third square.

31.

W. The knight at his king's fourth square.

B. The knight at his king's bishop's fourth square.

32.

W. The rook takes the knight.

B. The pawn takes the rook.

33.

W. The knight at the white queen's third
square.

B. The king's bishop's pawn one move, or
any where: the game being lost.

34.

W. The king's pawn one move.

B. The king's rook's at its queen's knight's
square.

35.

W. The bishop gives check.

B. The king retires, having but one place.

36.

W. The knight gives check.

B. The king removes.

37.

W. The knight at the black queen's square
discovering check.

B. The king moves where he can.

38.

W. The king's pawn making a queen, gives
checkmaet in the mean time.

There requires no animadversions no the moves of
this back game, they being almost all the same as in the
first game.

E

SECOND BACK GAME.

Beginning from the Thirty-seventh Move.

~~~~~

37.

W. The king's pawn gives check.

B. The king at his bishop's square.

38.

W. The rook at its queen's rook's square.

B. The rook gives check at the white queen's knight's square.

39.

W. The rook takes the rook.

B. The knight retakes the rook.

40.

W. The king at his rook's second square.

B. The knight at the white queen's bishop's third square.

41.

W. The knight at his king's bishop's fourth square.

B. The knight at the white king's fourth square.

42.

W. The king takes the pawn.

B. The rook at its king's knight's fourth square.

43.

W. The king's pawn one move, and gives check.

B. The king at his bishop's second square.

44.

W. The bishop gives check at the black king's third square.

B. The king takes the bishop.

45.

W. The king's pawn makes a queen, and wins the game.

CUNNINGHAM'S GAMBIT.

~~~~~

1.

White. The king's pawn two moves.
Black. The same.

2.

W. The king's bishop's pawn two moves.
B. The king's pawn takes the pawn.

3.

W. The king's knight at his bishop's third square.
B. The king's bishop at his king's second square.

4.

W. The king's bishop at his queen's bishop's fourth square.
B. The king's bishop gives check.

5.

W. The king's knight's pawn one move.
B. The pawn takes the pawn.

6.

W. The king castles.
B. The pawn takes the rook's pawn, and gives check.

7.

W. The king at his rook's square.

B. The king's bishop at his third square *(a)*.

8.

W. The king's pawn one move.

B. The queen's pawn two steps *(b)*.

9.

W. The king's pawn takes the bishop.

B. The king's knight takes the pawn.

10.

W. The king's bishop at his queen's knight's third square.

B. The queen's bishop at his king's third square.

11.

W. The queen's pawn one move *(c)*.

B. The king's rook's pawn one move *(d)*.

12.

W. The queen's bishop at his king's bishop's fourth square.

B. The queen's bishop's pawn two steps.

13.

W. The queen's bishop takes the pawn next to his king.

B. The queen's knight at his bishop's third square.

14.

W. The queen's knight at his queen's second
square.

B. The king's knight at the white king's
knight's fourth square (e).

15.

W. The queen at her king's second square (f).

B. The knight takes the bishop.

16.

W. The queen takes the knight.

B. The queen at her knight's square (g).

17.

W. The queen takes the queen (h).

B. The rook takes the queen.

18.

W. The queen's rook at its king's square.

B. The king at his queen's second square.

19.

W. The king's knight gives check.

B. The knight takes the knight.

20.

W. The queen's rook takes the knight.

B. The king at his queen's third square.

21.

W. The king's rook at its king's square.

B. The queen's knight's pawn two steps.

22.

W. The queen's bishop's pawn one step.

B. The queen's rook at its king's square.

23.

W. The queen's rook's pawn two steps.

B. The queen's rook's pawn one step.

24.

W. The knight at his king's bishop's third square.

B. The king's knight's pawn two steps.

25.

W. The king at his knight's second square.

B. The king's bishop's pawn one move *(i)*.

26.

W. The queen's rook at its king's second square.

B. The king's rook's pawn one step.

27.

W. The queen's rook's pawn takes the pawn.

B. The pawn retakes the pawn.

28.

W. The king's rook at its queen's rook's square.

B. The queen's rook at her home *(k)*.

29.

W. The king's rook returns to its king's square.

B. The bishop at his queen's second square.

30.

W. The queen's pawn one move..

B. The queen's bishop's pawn one move.

31.

W. The bishop at his queen's bishop's second square.

B. The king's rook's pawn one move *(l)*.

32.

W. The king's rook at his home.

B. The king's rook at its fourth square *(m)*.

33.

W. The queen's knight's pawn one move.

B. The queen's rook at its king's rook's square.

34.

W. The queen's knight's pawn one move.

B. The king's knight's pawn one move.

35.

W. The knight at his queen's second square,

B. The king's rook at its king's knight's fourth square.

36.

W. The king's rook at its king's bishop's square.

B. The king's knight's pawn one move.

37.

W. The rook takes the pawn and gives check.

B. The king at his queen's bishop's second square.

38.

W. The king's rook at the black king's knight's third square.

B. The king's rook's pawn gives check.

39.

W. The king at his knight's square.

B. The king's knight's pawn one move.

40.

W. The rook takes the rook.

B. The rook's pawn gives check.

41.

W. The king takes the knight's pawn.

B. The rook's pawn makes a queen, and gives check.

42.

W. The king at his bishop's second square.

B. The rook gives check at its king's bishop's square.

43.

W. The king at his third square.

B. The queen gives check at the white king's rook's third square.

44.

W. The knight covers the check having no
other way.

B. The queen takes the knight, and afterwards the rook, and gives mate in two
moves after.

BACK GAME.

Beginning of the Seventh Move of this Gambit.

~~~~

7

White. THE king at his rook's square.

Black. The bishop at his king's second square.

8.

W. The king's bishop takes the pawn, and gives check.

B. The king takes the bishop.

9.

W. The king's knight at the black king's fourth square, giving double check.

B. The king at his third square, any where else he loses his queen.

10.

W. The queen gives check at her king's knight's fourth square.

B. The king takes the knight.

11.

W. The queen gives check at the black king's bishop's fourth square.

B. The king at his queen's third square.

12.

W. The queen gives check-mate at the black queen's fourth square.

A SEQUEL

TO THE

BACK - GAME.

In case your adversary refuses taking your bishop
with his king, at the Eighth Move of
this Back-Game.

~~~~~~~

8.

White. THE king's bishop takes the pawn,
and gives check.

Black. The king at his bishop's square.

9.

W. The king's knight at the black king's
fourth square.

B. The king's knight at his king's bishop's
third square.

10.

W. The king's bishop at his queen's knight's
third square.

B. The queen at her king's square.

11.

W. The king's knight at the black king's
bishop's second square.

B. The rook at her knight's square.

12.

W. The king's pawn one move.

B. The queen's pawn two moves.

13.

W. The pawn takes the knight.

B. The pawn retakes the pawn.

14.

W. The bishop takes the pawn.

B. The queen's bishop at the white king's knight's fourth square.

15.

W. The queen at her king's square.

B. The queen's bishop at her king's rook's fourth square.

16.

W. The queen's pawn two steps *(a)*.

B. The bishop takes the knight.

17.

W. The queen's bishop gives check.

B. The rook covers the check.

18.

W. The knight at his queen's bishop's third square.

B. The bishop takes the bishop.

(a) This piece is sacrificed only to shorten the game.

F

19.

W. The knight retakes the bishop.

B. The queen at her king's bishop's second square.

20.

W. The knight takes the bishop.

B. The queen takes the knight.

21.

W. The queen takes the queen.

B. The king takes the queen.

22.

W. The bishop takes the rook, and with the superiority of a rook, besides a good situation, will easily win the game.

REFLECTIONS

ON

GAME THE FIRST.

~~~~~~

(*a*) This pawn is played two moves, for two very important reasons; the first is, to hinder your adversary's king's bishop to play upon your king's bishop's pawn : and the second, to put the strength of your pawns in the middle of the exchequer, which is of great consequence to attain the making of a queen.

(*b*) When you find your game in the present situation, viz. one of your pawns at your king's fourth square, and one at your queen's fourth square, you must push neither of them before your adversary proposes to change one for the other : in this case you are to push forwards the attacked pawn. It is to be observed that pawns, when sustained in a front line, hinder very much the adversary's pieces to enter in your game, or take an advantageous post. This rule may serve for all other pawns thus situated.

(*c*) If instead of retiring his bishop, he

gives you check with it, you are to cover the check with your bishop in order to retake his bishop with your knight, in case he takes your bishop; your knight will then defend your king's pawn, otherwise unguarded. But probably he will not take your bishop, because a good player strives to keep his king's bishop as long as possible.

(d) You must not early play your knight's at your bishop's third square, before the bishop's pawn has moved two steps, because the knight proves an hindrance to the motion of the pawn.

(e) Your bishop retires to avoid being attacked by the black queen's pawn, which would force you to take his pawn with yours; this would very much diminish the strength of your game, and spoil entirely the project already mentioned, and observed in the first and second reflections. *Vide a* and *b.*

(f) He plays this pawn to give an opening to his king's rook; and this cannot be hindered, whether you take his pawn or not.

(g) If you should take the pawn offered to you, instead of playing your queen, you would be guilty of a great fault, because your royal pawn would then lose its line;

whereas, if he takes your king's pawn, that of your queen supplies the place, and you may afterwards sustain it with that of your king's bishop's pawn : These two pawns will undoubtedly win the game, because they can now no more be separated without the loss of a piece, or one of them will make a queen, as will be seen by the sequel of this game. Moreover, it is of no small consequence to play your queen in that place for two reasons; the first, to support and defend your king's bishop's pawn; and secondly, to sustain your queen's bishop, which being taken, would oblige you to retake his bishop with the above-mentioned last pawn; and thus your best pawns would have been totally divided, and of course the game indubitably lost.

(h) He takes the pawn to pursue his project, which is to give an opening to his king's rook, and make it fit for action.

(i) He plays his bishop to protect his queen's pawn, and with a view to push afterwards that of his queen's bishop's.

Observe he might have taken your bishop without prejudice to his scheme, but he chuses rather to let you take his, in order to get an opening for his queen's rook, though he suffers to have his knight's pawn doubled by it; but you are again to observe, that a double pawn is no ways disadvantageous when surrounded by three or four other pawns. However, to avoid criticism, this will be seen in the back-game, beginning from this twelfth move, to which you are sent after the party is over; the black bishop will then take your bishop; it will also be shewn, that, playing well on both sides, it will make no alteration in the case. The king's pawn, together with the queen's, or the king's bishop's pawn, well played and well sustained, will certainly win the game.

N. B. In regard to these back-games I shall make them only upon the most essential moves; for if I were to make them upon every move it would be an endless work.

(k) Your king's pawn being as yet in no danger, your knight attacks his bishop, in order to take it or have it removed.

(l) As it is always dangerous to let the adversary's king's bishop batter the line of your king's bishop's pawn; and as it is likewise the most dangerous piece to form an attack, it is only necessary to oppose him by times to your queen's bishop, but you must get rid of that piece as soon as a convenient occasion offers.

(m) You chuse to castle on the king's side in order to strengthen and protect your king's bishop's pawn, which you will advance two steps as soon as your king's pawn is attacked.

(n) He is forced to play this pawn, to hinder you from pushing your king's bishop's pawns upon his queen.

(o) This king's rook's pawn is played to unite all your pawns together, and push them afterwards with vigour.

(p) He plays this pawn to hinder your knight entering in his game, and forcing his queen to remove; were he to play otherwise, your pawns would have an open field.

(q) You play this knight to enable yourself to push your king's bishop's pawn next; it will be then supported by three pieces, the bishop, the rook, and the knight.

(r) He plays this knight to hinder your project by breaking the strength of your pawns, which he would undoubtedly do by pushing his king's knight's pawn; but you break his design by changing your rook for his knight.

(s) You play your rook to protect your king's pawn, who would remain in the lurch as soon as you push your king's bishop's pawn.

(t) The queen returns to hinder the check-mate, now ready departed.

(u) Were you not to take with your pawn, your first project, laid in the beginning of the game, would be reduced to nothing, and you would run the risk of losing the game.

(w) He offers to change queens in order to break your scheme of giving him check-mate with your queen and bishop.

(x) You are to observe when your bishop runs upon white, you must strive to put your pawn always upon black, because then your bishop serves to drive away your adversary's king or rook when between your pawns; the same when your bishop runs black, to have then your pawns upon white. Few players have made this remark, though a very essential one.

(y) As his king may retire at his bishop's square, it is necessary to send you to a second back-game, which will shew you how to proceed in this case.

REFLECTIONS

ON

CUNNINGHAM'S GAMBIT.

~~~~

(a) If instead of playing this bishop at his third square he had played it at his king's second square, you had won the game in a few moves, which you will see by my first back-game, beginning from this seventh move.

(b) Without a sacrifice of this bishop he could not win the game : but, losing it, for three pawns, he must by a good managemen· of them become your conqueror. The ver· strength of those three pawns, (provided he doth not be too hasty, in pushing them for· wards, and that they be always well sustained by his pieces) will win the game in spite o your best defence.

(c) If you had pushed this pawn two step you had given to his knights a free entry

x

your game, which would have lost you the party very soon. Indeed it is so extremely obvious, that it is unnecessary to make it the subject of a second back-game, which I at first intended.

(d) This move is of great consequence to him, because it hinders you from attacking his king's knight with your queen's bishop which would have enabled you to separate his pawns by changing one of your rooks for one of his knights, and in this case the advantage of the game would have turned on your side.

(e) He plays this knight to take your queen's bishop, which would prove very incommodious to him in case he should castle on his queen's side. It is here proper to observe again, as a general rule, that if the strength of your game consists in pawns, the best way is to take the adversary's bishop as soon as possible, because they can stop the advancing of the pawns much better than the rooks.

(f) Not knowing how to save your bishop without doing worse, you play your queen to take his place again when taken; for if you had played it at your king's bishop's fourth square to hinder the check of his knight, he would have pushed his king's knight's pawn upon your said bishop, and would have made you lose the game immediately.

(g) If he had played his queen any where else, she would have been cramped : therefore he offers to change, that in case you refuse he may place her at her third square, where she not only would have been safe, but extremely well posted.

(h) If you did not take his queen, your game would be still in a worse condition.

(i) If he had pushed this pawn two steps, you had gained his queen's pawn, taking it with your bishop, this would have mended your game very much.

(k) One must always strive to hinder the adversary from doubling his rooks, particularly when there is an opening in the game, therefore he proposes immediately to change one for the other.

(l) He plays this pawn to push afterwards that of his king's knight's upon your knight, with an intention to force it from his post; but if he had pushed his knight's pawn before he played this, you must have posted your knight at your king's rook's fourth square,

and by this means you would have stopped
the progress of all his pawns.

(*m*) If instead of playing this, he had given
check with his rook's pawn, he would have
played ill, and entirely against the instruction
given in the former part.

THE END.

H. Bryer, Printer, Bridge Street, Blackfriars, London.

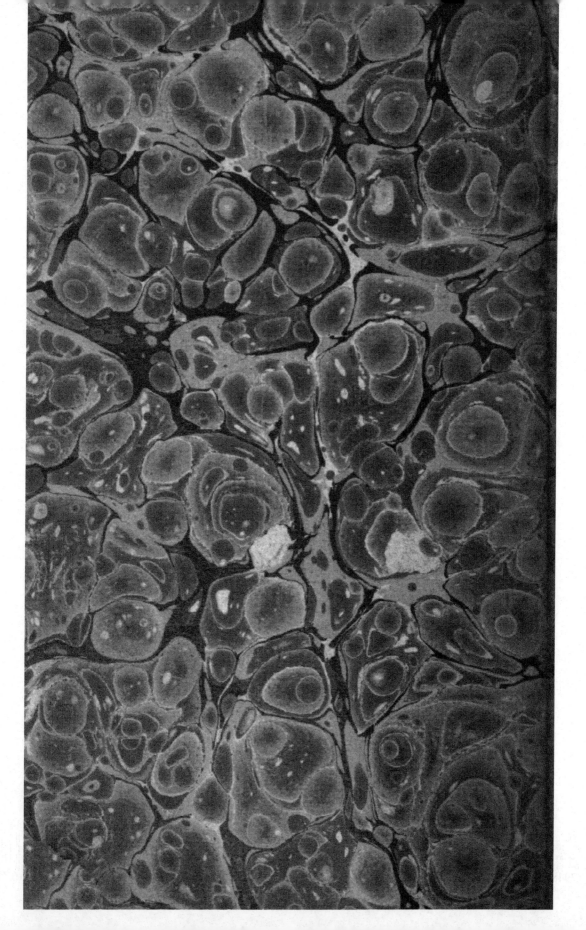

CPSIA information can be obtained
at www.ICGtesting.com
Printed in the USA
LVOW05s1547191216

517948LV00020B/814/P